The Book
of
Tah

Commentary and Compilation
by
Zahir Mahmood

Edited by
Hafiz Muhammad Nawaz Daud

Cover Design and Illustrations
by
Javed Khan

First Edition 2000

Published by Inter-Islam Publishing Company
5 Garendon Street, Leicester.

Contents

All praise be to Allah the Lord of the Worlds and peace and blessings be upon His chosen prophet Mu-hammad and may Allah be pleased with his Companions and those who follow them in a good manner until the Day of Judgement.

No book is devoid of usefulness; in fact, a book is an increase in knowledge, which the individual will find if and when he needs it, for there, is no way for the individual to retain all the knowledge in which he specialises. And since there is no way to accomplish this it follows that books are delightful storehouses for the individual seeking knowledge had it not been for the testimony of books, the claim of both the scholar and ignoramus would be on par.

Ibn Hazm

Fiqh (Jurisprudence) and the *Fuqahā'* (Jurists)

The quintessence of Islamic teaching is the Qur'ān and *sunna* and the means of understanding these primary sources is accurately crystallised through the science of *fiqh*. *Fiqh* is the eyesight whilst the Qur'ān and *sunna* are the light. Eyesight is an indispensable tool for deriving benefit from light; in its absence light is of little use and vice-versa. Similarly, it is through the implementation of *fiqh* that one is able to extract the finer implications and subtleties articulated in the Qur'ān and *sunna*.

Fiqh literally means to comprehend and understand. In early Islamic history, the term included legal, ethical and theological norms. *Fiqh* dealing with creed was termed *al-fiqh al-akbar*, (Imām Abū Ḥanīfa's book entitled *al-Fiqh al-akbar* and his definition of *fiqh* bear testimony to this), and the term *faqīh* denoted equally a 'jurist' and 'theologian.'

Later definitions, such as Imām al-Shāfiʿī's, begin to portray a dichotomy between legal theory and theology: 'Knowledge that is discerned from the detailed proofs (the Qur'ān, *sunna, ijmā*[c] (consensus) and *qiyās* (analogical deduction)) regarding norms for actions in the *sharī*[c]*a.* (*al-Fiqh al-islāmī wa adillatuh* p.16)

The clause 'discerned from the detailed proofs' precludes the layman from indulging in deriving *fiqh.* The successful derivation of *fiqh* requires the ability to discern rulings from the Qur'ān and *sunna, ijmā*[c] (consensus) and *qiyās* (analogical deduction). These derivations entail a complexity that a layman is ignorant of. If he does possess the ability, then he neither belongs to the laity, nor to ordinary scholarship, but to the higher category of the jurists.

Fiqh (comprehension) has varying levels, the optimum level consists of direct inspiration from Allah, to which the words of the Prophet (may Allah bless him and grant him peace) attest, "For whomsoever Allah wishes good he endows him with *fiqh* of the religion." Ibn Ḥajr commenting upon this tradition (*ḥadīth*) remarks, "In this narration there is a clear elucidation of the superiority of the [c]*ulamā* over the laity and that of *fiqh* in religion above all other sciences. (*Fatḥ al-Bārī* 1/217)

In another tradition the Prophet (may Allah bless him and grant him peace) said, "May Allah keep fresh one who hears my words, preserves them and then conveys them to those who have not heard them. At times the one carrying *fiqh* has no *fiqh* himself, and at times the one carrying *fiqh* conveys it to one who has more *fiqh* than himself." Ḥākim and Dhahabī state, "This narration fulfils the conditions of Bukhārī and Muslim," and the former has declared the narration as *mashhūr* (well-known).

The narration delineates that a fundamental purpose of the propagation of traditions is the inference of *fiqh* from it. Furthermore, the initial bearer of the traditions may himself not possess the required tools to derive *fiqh*, whilst a later bearer may, and his derivations may benefit Muslims. It is here that a distinction is drawn between the *muḥaddithūn* and the *fuqahā'*.

The former place emphasis on memorising texts, chains of transmission, biographies of the transmitters etc, whilst the latter derive from the traditions their deeper implications.

This distinction between the *fuqahā'* and the *muḥaddathūn* (traditionists) reaches as far back as to the time of the *Ṣaḥāba* (may Allah be pleased with them). Eminent compilers of traditions such as Abū Hurayra (may Allah be pleased with him), who despite transmitting more traditions than many other *Ṣaḥāba* (may Allah be pleased with them), very rarely issued formal legal rulings (*fatāwa*), and despite his immense knowledge of traditions was not regarded as a *faqihī* among the *Ṣaḥāba*.

Further clarification of this distinction is Muḥammad Rawās al-Qal^cahjī's *Silsila al-mawsū^ca fiqh al-salaf,* compendiums illustrating the legal rulings of distinguished *Ṣaḥāba* (may Allah be pleased with them). The work dealing with the *fiqh* of Abū Hurayra (may Allah be pleased with him) is in total a fifth compared with the rulings of other distinguished *Ṣaḥāba* (may Allah be pleased with them), who transmitted far fewer traditions than Abū Hurayra (may Allah be pleased with him).

Further illustrations can be found in the following examples:

A person rebuked Imām Aḥmad b. Ḥanbal for leaving the circles of Sufyān b. al-ᶜUyayna for that of Imām al-Shāfiᶜī. Imām Aḥmad replied, "Keep silent! If a tradition with a higher chain eludes you, then you will acquire it through a lower chain. However, if the insight of this young man passes you by, I fear you will never come across it again." (*al-Rafᶜ wa al-takmīl fī al-jarḥ wa al-taᶜdīl,* p.71)

On another occasion Imām Aḥmad said, "Knowledge of traditions and the *fiqh* thereof are more beloved to me than the memorisation of traditions." (*al-Rafᶜ wa al-takmīl fī al-jarḥ wa al-taᶜdīl,* p.70) ᶜAlī b. al-Madīnī said, "The most noblest of sciences is the knowledge of *fiqh* within the *aḥādīth.*" (*Maqām Abī Ḥanīfa,* p.52)

The deep insight and intellectual excellence needed to attain the status of a *faqīh* ensured that the *fuqahā'* remained considerably fewer in number than the *Muḥaddithūn.* Ḥāfiz al-Ramhurmizī has stated in *al-Muḥaddith al-fāṣil bain al-rāwī al-wāᶜī,* with his own chain of transmission from Anas b. Sirīn that, "I came to Kufa where I found four thousand seeking traditions and four hundred had become *fuqahā'.*'" (*al-Taᶜlīq al-mumajjad ᶜalā Muwaṭṭā Muḥammad,* 1/20)

Notwithstanding their excellence in *ḥadīth,* many eminent *muḥaddithūn* of the 'Golden Generations' imbibed the *fiqh* of the great *fuqahā'* of their time. From amongst those eminent *muḥaddithūn* who adhered to the opinions of the eponym of the Ḥanafī school of thought, Abū Ḥanīfa, were eminent figures such as Wakīᶜ b. al-Jarāḥ, a teacher of Aḥmad b. Ḥanbal, Isḥāq b. Rahwai, Abū Bakr b. Abī Shayba, ᶜAlī b. al-Madīnī and Yaḥyā b. Maᶜīn.

Imām Aḥmad b. Ḥanbal said, "I have never seen anyone equal to Wakīᶜ in knowledge, memorisation, acquaintance with the chains of transmission and chapter headings (*abwāb*)." (*Tahdhīb al-kamāl,* 30/473)

Yaḥyā b. Maᶜīn said, "I swear by Allah I have never seen anyone other than Wakīᶜ narrate solely for the sake of Allah, nor anyone who had memorised more than him. He in his era was like Awzaiᶜī was in his." (*Tahdhīb al-kamāl,* 30/475)

Yaḥyā b. Maᶜīn also said, "I have never seen anyone more virtuous than Wakīᶜ." He was asked if Wakīᶜ was even more virtuous than Ibn al-Mubārak. He replied, "Ibn al-Mubārak is virtuous, but I have never seen anyone more virtuous than Wakīᶜ, he would face the *Qibla* and memorise traditions, he would fast successively and issue *fatāwa* according to the opinion of Abū Ḥanīfā." (*Tahdhīb al-kamāl,* 30/474)

Another from amongst these illustrious scholars was Yaḥyā b. Ma[c]īn, a teacher of many well-known scholars including Imām Bukhārī, Muslim, Abū Dā'ūd, and Abū Ḥātim al-Razī to name just a few.

Muḥammad b. Naṣr al-Ṭabrī reported, "I heard Yaḥyā b. Ma[c]īn state, 'With these hands of mine I have written a million traditions.'" (*Tahdhīb al-kamāl,* 31/548)

[c]Abd al-Khāliq said, "I said to Ibn Rūmī, 'I have heard a traditionist say, 'Yaḥyā b. Ma[c]īn the one who the sun has not risen upon greater than (in traditions) narrated to me.' He replied, "Why the surprise? I heard [c]Alī b. al-Madīnī say, 'I have never seen amongst the people one equal to him.'" (*Tahdhīb al-kamāl,* 31/553)

Imām Dhahabī has stated regarding Yaḥyā b. Ma[c]īn that he was a staunch Ḥanafī, notwithstanding the fact that he was a *muḥaddith.* (*al-Kanz al-matawārī,* 1/159)

Another eminent scholar who followed the opinions of Imām Abū Ḥanīfa was Yaḥyā al-Qaṭṭan, a teacher of Aḥmad b. Ḥanbal, Sufyān al-Thawrī, Sufyān b. al-[c]Uyaina, Sh[c]uba b. al-Ḥajjāj and [c]Ali b. al-Madīnī.

Abū Ṭālib reported from Aḥmad b. Ḥanbal that he said, "I have never seen anyone like Yaḥyā b. Sa[c]īd, in his era there was none equal to him." (*Tahdhīb al-Kamāl,* 31/337)

Zakarīya b. Yaḥyā al-Sājī said, "I heard [c]Alī b. al-Madīnī say, 'I have never come across anyone who was more knowledgeable regarding the biographies of narrators than Yaḥyā b. Sa[c]īd al-Qaṭṭan.'" (*Tahdhīb al-kamāl,* 31/336)

An indication of how a revered scholar such as Yaḥyā b. Saᶜīd al-Qaṭṭan accepted and acted upon the *fiqh* of Abū Ḥanīfa is evident from the following statement. Saᶜīd al-Qāḍī states, "I heard Yaḥyā b. Maᶜīn say, 'Yaḥyā b. Saᶜīd al-Qaṭṭan said, 'We do not belie Allah when we say that we have never heard an opinion better than that of Abū Ḥanīfa's, and we have accepted the majority of his statements.''" (*al-Taᶜlīq al-mumajjad ᶜalā Muwaṭṭā Muḥammad,* 1/16)

These eminent *muḥaddathūn* ceded the arduous task of drawing *fiqhī* rulings to those who were more adequately equipped to take up this demanding intellectual challenge. This approach was adopted throughout the Golden Generations, a period which witnessed the flourishing of many schools of thought; the majority of which did not survive due to a lack of preservation by their followers. Imām al-Shāfiᶜī stated: "Laith was a greater *faqīh* than Mālik but his students wasted him (through not preserving his teachings)." (*Siyār iᶜlām al-nubalā'*, 8/156)

Those schools which were preserved throughout the centuries up until the present day were subjected to rigorous refinement and amendment by the scores of scholars who adhered to them. In each century, using the *uṣūl al-fiqh* (principles of jurisprudence) of the school, casuistic conflict solutions (*masā'il*) were deduced to deal with the exigencies of the time.

A testimony to the acceptance of these schools of thought is the unfaltering adherence they enjoyed throughout the centuries. It would be no exaggeration to state that the overwhelming majority of Muslims avidly adopted these schools. It is only of late, due to a moral and scholarly degeneration in the *ummah,* that individuals have begun to excoriate the schools and their followers. It is therefore important that whilst facing antagonism, one adhering to the *fiqh* of one of the great Imams must also adopt their sublime manners, tolerance, and the deep respect and love that they exhibited for their Muslim brothers, even if they contravened their personal position. May Allah guide them and us, for they are our brothers in the *Dīn,* and

'None of you can be a true believer until he desires for his brother what he wishes for himself.'

Disputation, according to Imām Ghazālī, is only valid if the following conditions are met:

1) Disputation is a communal obligation (*al-farḍ al-kifāya*); before one may practise it he must have already fulfilled the individual obligations (*al-farḍ al-ᶜayn*).
2) The purpose of disputation is to seek the truth; and it is justified only when there is not a more important community obligation that should be performed.
3) Disputation is justified only in the case of a *mujtahid*, capable of arriving at his own legal opinion and who is not bound by the opinions of any school of law.
4) Disputation is justified only in cases that are likely to be of actual occurrence.
5) Disputation should be held privately, rather than in public assemblies in the presence of notables and men of power and influence.
6) In disputation the aim should be to seek the truth regardless of which of the two adversaries finds it.
7) Disputation should be free of certain restrictive rules of dialectic, such as preventing the adversaries shifting from one argument to another.
8) A disputant should dispute with an opponent from whose knowledge he expects to benefit, one who occupies himself with legitimate religious knowledge.

After presenting his eight conditions Imām Ghazālī states that there are others of minor importance, "but in these eight conditions there is that which will show you the difference between those who dispute for the sake of Allah, and those who do so for an ulterior motive." (*The Non-Ashāᶜrite Shāfīᶜism of Abū Hāmid Ghazālī*)

The Author

The author is Abū al-Ikhlāṣ al-Ḥasan b. ʿAmmār b. ʿAlī b. Yūsuf he was born in Shrunbalāl in 994 A/H. He commenced his studies at the prestigious seat of learning, al-Azhar, Cairo, under the patronage of some of the most eminent scholars of his time. He himself later became a scholar of great repute and a copious writer, whose works exceed fifty in number. The Shaykh passed away in 1069 A/H.

Notes On The Text

The *Nūr al-īḍāḥ* is a classical text on sacred law, and for generations has been one of the most widely taught texts used to transmit Ḥanafī *fiqh*. Generations of scholars and layman alike have been taught the *Nūr al-īḍāḥ*, which gives them sufficient grounding in the basic *masā'il* they encounter daily.

About This Compilation

Throughout this work, the main text has been based on the *Nūr al-Īḍāḥ*, whilst any text in brackets has been taken from reliable Ḥanāfī sources and commentaries on the *Nūr al-Īḍāḥ*. These sources are sometimes mentioned in abbreviation, before the closing bracket. Bracketed commentaries marked by 'Z' indicate a synopsis not a full translation from supplementary works so as to allow more leeway in explaining complex rulings within the text. I have refrained from inserting anything from my part except what was essential for the clarification of the text. A number of contemporary *fatāwa* have been taken from Muftī Rashīd Aḥmad's *Aḥsan al-fatāwa.* The chapter regarding the rulings of the water from the well has been omitted because of its irrelevance to the society for which this book has been compiled. Similarly, other rulings that may be a source of confusion for the reader without the assistance of a teacher have also been omitted.

Finally, I acknowledge that there are far more able individuals than myself to undertake this task, and therefore no claim is made that this work is free from error. Yet despite my shortcomings, I have deemed it important to present this work because of the paucity of suitable material on the fundamental subject of *ṭahāra* in the English language.

Zahir Mahmood,
Birmingham, England,
26 Rabīᶜ al-Awwal 1421/27 June 2000

Abbreviations

ai = *Ashraf al-īḍāḥ sharḥ nūr al-īḍāḥ*

Ahf = *Aḥsan al-fatāwa*

Mf = *Marāqī al-falāḥ sharḥ nūr al-īḍāḥ*

Mf+t = *Ḥāshīya ʿalā marāqī al-falāḥ sharḥ nūr al-īḍāḥ*

Lub = *Lubāb fī sharḥ al-kitāb*

Definitions of the *Uṣūl al-Fiqh* Terminologies to be found in this Work

1.1 While the majority of jurists regard *farḍ* and *wājib* as synonymous, the Ḥanafis draw a clear distinction between the two. Isḥāq b. Ibrahīm al-Shāshī in defining the two states, "Linguistically *farḍ* means to decree, whilst in the *Sharī^{c}a,* it denotes that which is delineated in such a manner that no increase or decrease is possible. The command of a *farḍ* is communicated by a definite *(qaṭ^{c}ī)* text wherein there is no ambiguity, clear and specific. To act upon it and to believe in it is binding… *wājib,* technically means that which is established by a text of an ambiguous or speculative (*zannī*) authority, such as an allegorically interpreted (*mu'awal*) verse."

The majority of jurists and Ḥanafīs agree that *farḍ* and *wājib* are both binding. *Farḍ* is communicated by a clear definite text with no ambiguity or speculation and *wājib* by a speculative text. As a consequence the obligation emanating from a *farḍ* is of a greater degree than that from a *wājib.* The omission of a *farḍ* invalidates the act, such as the unanimous view of the jurists that the omission of the stay at *^{c}Arafa* (def: 5.12 (s)), which is a *farḍ* act, renders one's *ḥajj* null and void. Whilst the omission of *sa^{c}ī* (pacing) between *al-Ṣaffa* and *al-Marwa* (def:

5.12 (t)), which is communicated by a speculative authority will not invalidate the *ḥajj.* Another distinction is that one who refuses to believe in a *farḍ* such as *ṣalāḥ* or *zakah* is rendered an unbeliever. However, the denial of believing in an obligation established by a speculative authority will not make one an unbeliever. (edited excerpts from *Ūṣūl al-fiqh,* p.23 and *Ūṣūl al-Shāshī,* p.172)

The term *wājib,* when used in a non-*Shari*^{c} context, has the connotation of 'necessary.' An example is '*al-qir'at wājib* ^{c}*alayk*' (it is necessary that you read). Whenever the term has occurred in this work, I have endeavoured to discern whether it is the *Shari*^{c} or non-*Shari*^{c} term that is implied. However, if I have failed to understand its precise connotation at any place, such discrepancies are from Satan and myself, for which I seek refuge in Allah and seek His and your pardon.

1.2 *Sunna mu*^{c}*akkada* (emphatic *sunna*) is an act upheld by the Prophet (may Allah bless him and grant him peace) perpetually whilst letting it be known that its performance is not *farḍ,* such as the two *rak*^{c}*ahs* before the *farḍ* of the *fajr* prayer and after *zuhr, maghrib* and ^{c}*ishā'.* The abandonment of a *sunna mu*^{c}*akkada* (emphatic *sunna*) is not punishable, but nevertheless the perpetrator will be reproached, because its omission would be tantamount to opposing that which the Prophet (may Allah bless him and grant him peace) perpetuated. (edited excerpts from *Ūṣūl al-fiqh,* p.31)

The giving of non-obligatory charity for one who is capable, the four *rak*^{c}*ahs* before ^{c}*aṣr* and ^{c}*ishā'* are *sunna ghayr mu*^{c}*akkada,* namely, actions which the Prophet (may Allah bless him and grant him peace) did not perform perpetually. (edited excerpts from *Ūṣūl al-fiqh,* p.31) It is also referred to as *mustaḥab.*

1.3 *Adāb* (sing: *adab*) is that which the Prophet (may Allah bless him and grant him peace) did only once or twice throughout his life. It is a rewardable act with no reproach for one who abandons it. It has also been defined as praiseworthy manners. (*Marāqī al-falāḥ,* p.111)

1.4 *Ḥarām* is an obligatory command from the Lawgiver demanding abstinence from something. It is communicated by a definite authority. Examples are eating the flesh of a dead animal, drinking alcohol, fornicating, adultery, unjustly killing someone and many others. (edited excerpts from *Ūṣūl al-fiqh,* p.33)

1.5 *Makrūh* according to the Ḥanafīs is a command for abstinence from something established by a speculative proof. It is divided into two categories, namely, *makrūh taḥrīm* and *makrūh tanzīh.* The former is closer to *ḥarām* and can also be defined as being in diametrical opposition to a *wājib. Makrūh tanzīh* is closer to *mubāḥ* and in diametrical opposition to a *mustaḥab.* (edited excerpts from *Ūṣūl al-fiqh,* p.36)

1.6 *Mubāḥ* is an allowance from the Lawgiver to a *mukallaf* (a competent person who is in full possession of his faculties) in performing or refraining from an act, such as eating or drinking. Shawkānī defined *mubāḥ* as that "upon which no commendation is shown upon its performance or omission." At times it is used to illustrate the permissibility of a generally prohibited act such as the statement 'The blood of an apostate is lawful (*mubāḥ*)' meaning there is no harm upon one who kills him. *Mubāḥ* is also referred to as *ḥalāl* and *jā'iz.* (edited excerpts from *Ūṣūl al-fiqh,* p.36)

1.7 Communal obligation (*al-farḍ al-kifāya*) is an obligation which is incurred upon all, without specifying those who should perform it. Its obligation upon all will be lifted if fulfilled by a few. Examples of *al-farḍ al-kifāya* are the funeral prayer, to enjoin good and forbid evil, furnishing definite proofs upon the existence of Allah etc. (*al-Mawsūᶜa al-fiqhīya,* (32/96))

Water

2.1 There are seven types of water with which cleanliness can be achieved:

(1) rainwater;
(2) seawater;
(3) river water;
(4) well water;
(5) water from melted ice;
(6) water from melted hail;
(7) and spring water.

2.2 Water (with regards to its states) can be one of five types:

(1) *Muṭlaq* (pure) water: water which is intrinsically pure and purifying for others but is not *makrūh* (def: 1.6) [Z: the last clause will become clearer whilst discussing the next type].

(2) Water which is intrinsically pure and purifying for others, but is *makrūh*. This is a small quantity of water (def: 2.2 (4)) from which a cat or a similar animal has partaken.

(3) Water which is intrinsically pure, but not purifying for others; that which has been used (*mustaᶜmal*) to remove a state of ritual impurity, or used for the sake of attaining rewards, such as *wuḍū'* performed afresh by one who already has *wuḍū'* with the intention of *wuḍū'* [Z: in order to obtain reward and not merely for the sake of cooling oneself down or removing dust from one's limbs, ai: p.8].

Water becomes used (*mustaᶜmal*) by its mere separation from the body.

[Z: If a *junbī* (one in a state of major ritual impurity) inserts his hand which is free from any apparent *najāsa* into a bowl of water, then that water will be rendered *musta^c^mal.* This is provided that other means of extracting the water are available. If there is no other means then the water shall remain *muṭlaq.* (def: 2.2 (1)), Ahf: 1/140].

Cleanliness cannot be attained by using water from a tree or fruit even if it has come forth without being squeezed. Nor can it be attained from water, which has lost its nature through being cooked or through the predominance of something else over it.

Predominance when water is mixed with a solid substance occurs when that water loses its thinness and liquidity, and thus such water no longer remains fit for *wuḍū'*.

When mixed with a solid substance, such as saffron, fruit and leaves of a tree, then the water shall continue to be purifying even though all its qualities [colour, smell and taste] have changed.

Predominance when water is mixed with a liquid, which has two qualities, is that one of these qualities becomes apparent in the water, such as milk, which has the qualities of colour and taste but not smell. Thereby, when water is mixed with a liquid that has three qualities, when two of these qualities become apparent in the water this signifies predominance, an example of such a liquid is vinegar.

Predominance when water is mixed with those liquids, which have no qualities, will be judged according to proportion such as in the case of used water or rose water from which the smell has diminished. Thus if two litres of used water are mixed with one litre of pure water, then *wuḍū'* is not permissible with it. It would be permissible if the proportion is to the contrary.

(4) Impure water: A small quantity of stagnant water in which *najāsa* (def: 10.1) has fallen. A small quantity of water is that amount which is less than ten by ten. [Z: Ten by ten in current measurements in a surface, the product of its width and length being 225ft or 20.9m]. It will be regarded impure [if *najāsa* falls into it] even though the signs of *najāsa* are not visible. The signs of *najāsa* are; taste, colour and smell.

[Z: The death of those animals which have no flowing blood does not make the water impure, whether they died in the water, or outside and thereafter were thrown into it. (Lub:1/22) Similarly the death of those animals which live in the water do not make it impure, such as fish, frogs or crayfish, Lub: 1/23].

(5) Water in whose quality of cleansing there is a doubt; from which a donkey or mule has drunk.

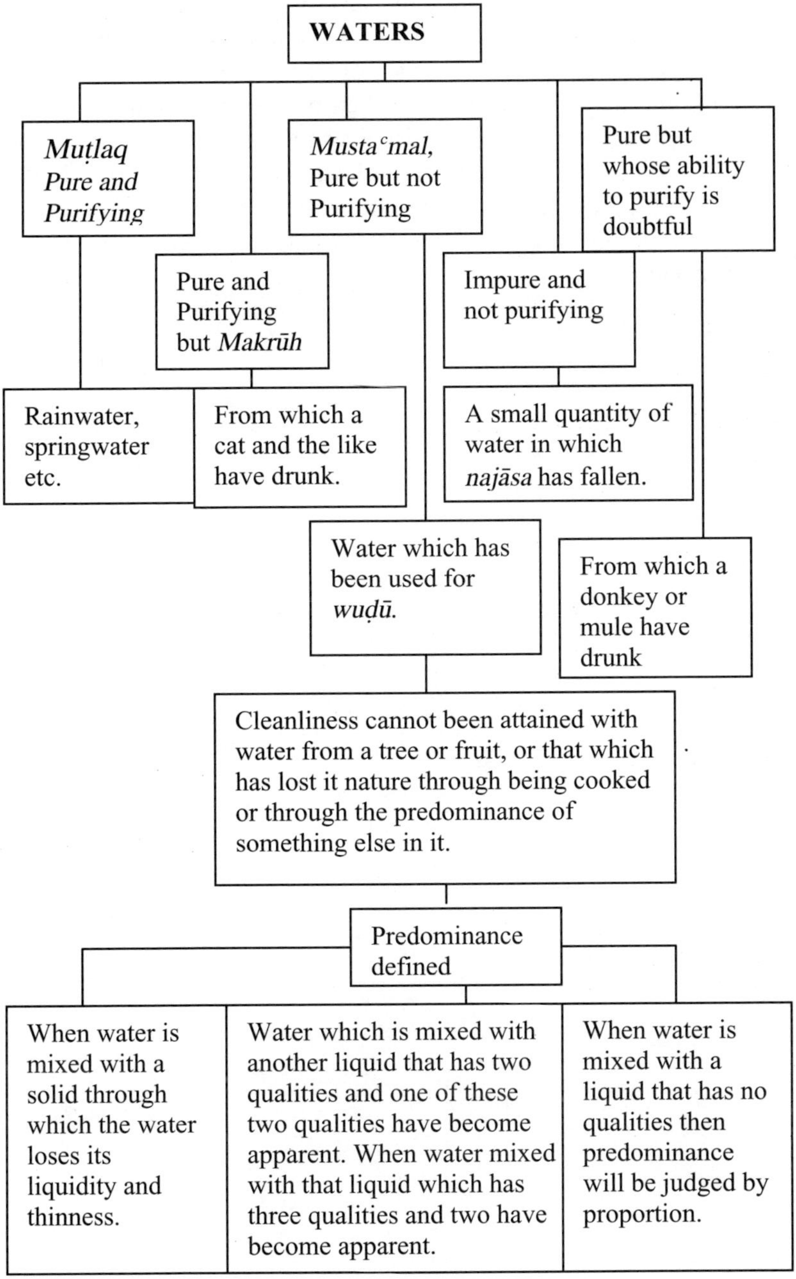
WATERS
Muṭlaq Pure and Purifying
Pure and Purifying but *Makrūh*
Musta^{c}mal, Pure but not Purifying
Impure and not purifying
Pure but whose ability to purify is doubtful
Rainwater, springwater etc.
From which a cat and the like have drunk.
A small quantity of water in which *najāsa* has fallen.
Water which has been used for *wuḍū.*
From which a donkey or mule have drunk
Cleanliness cannot been attained with water from a tree or fruit, or that which has lost it nature through being cooked or through the predominance of something else in it.
Predominance defined
When water is mixed with a solid through which the water loses its liquidity and thinness.
Water which is mixed with another liquid that has two qualities and one of these two qualities have become apparent. When water mixed with that liquid which has three qualities and two have become apparent.
When water is mixed with a liquid that has no qualities then predominance will be judged by proportion.

When some pure pots of water are mixed with impure ones, but the majority are pure, then one is obliged to discern the pure ones if intending to do *wuḍū'* or drink water. If on the other hand the majority are impure then one is exempted from doing this, unless one intends to drink water, [because as a substitute for *wuḍū'* one may perform *tayammum,* Mf: p.76]. If pure and impure clothes are mixed then one is required to discern the pure from the impure regardless whether the majority are pure or impure.

Su'r (Remnant Water)

3.1 When an animal drinks from a small quantity of water (def: 2.2 (4)) the remaining water is then known as *su'r*. This is of four types:

(1) The water is clean and cleansing, e.g. from which a human, horse or those animals whose meat is lawful for consumption have partaken. [Z: If after consuming something unlawful in the *sharī^{c}a* such as wine, pork etc, one immediately drinks some water his *su'r* will be impure, ai: p.14].

[Z: It is *makrūh* to partake from the *su'r* of such a person through whose *su'r* one attains sensual pleasure, with the exception of a married couple, Mf+t: p.20].

(2) Impure water, its usage is unlawful, e.g. water from which a dog, swine or any other predatory animal such as a cheetah or wolf has partaken.

(3) The usage of what is *makrūh* whilst other (pure) water exists, such as the *su'r* of a (domesticated) cat [Z: which is *makrūh* if one possesses other food or water. However, for a hungry destitute it is permitted. Whilst, the *su'r* of a wild cat is impure, Mf: p.74]; as is the *su'r* of an undomesticated chicken [because of the possibility that it may have inserted its beak into impurity, Mf: p.74]; the *su'r* of predatory birds such as a hawk, falcon or kite is *makrūh,* [if the bird is encaged and the owner is sure that there is no *najāsa* upon its beak, then it is not *makrūh. Sharḥ fatḥ al-qadīr,* 1/113]. Similarly, the *su'r* of a rat is *makrūh.*

(4) Water whose quality of purifying is doubtful, from which a mule or donkey has partaken. If no other water exists then one should do both *wuḍū'* and *tayammum* and then pray.

Istinjā' (Cleansing the Private Parts after answering the Call of Nature)

4.1 It is compulsory that one ensures that the drops of urine have ceased, and that one's heart is content according to one's general habit, either by walking, coughing, lying down or any other method. [Z: Other methods, which may be used, are to gently press one's penis or place a tissue under one's lower garment and take a brisk walk, methods may vary in accordance with the severity of one's problem].

4.2 It is unlawful to perform *wuḍū'* until one is content that the drops of urine have ceased. [Z: If Satan is continually creating doubts about the leakage of urine, then these doubts should be ignored. One should sprinkle some water over the genitals and the lower garment. Thereafter, when afflicted with doubt the wetness felt may be regarded as the sprinkled water. This is in the case of a doubt, but if one is sure that the wetness is urine then the required measures for purification will have to be undertaken, Mf+t: p.29].

4.3 It is *sunna* to perform *istinjā'* from any *najāsa* that exits from the front or back passage of the private parts and has not spread past the orifice. However, it is *wājib* if the *najāsa* has spread past the orifice and is equivalent to the size of a *dirham*. And *farḍ* if it has spread more than a *dirham*. [Z: A *dirham* is approximately the size of a British fifty pence coin].

4.4 To wash away whatever (*najāsa*) is in the orifice whilst bathing to remove a state of major ritual impurity, menstruation and postnatal bleeding is *farḍ*. Even though the *najāsa* may be of a small quantity.

4.5 It is *sunna* to do *istinjā'* with a cleansing stone or the like [Z: all things pure and not valued or venerated can be used in place of a stone, Mf+t: p.30]. To perform *istinjā'* with water is preferred. The best is to combine both water and stone, first by wiping with the stone and then washing. To use only water or to wipe with stones alone is also permissible.

[Z: Paper being a source of attaining knowledge is a venerated item, thus to perform *istinjā'* with it is *makrūh tanzīh.* Whilst the usage of toilet paper which is specifically made for the purpose of *istinjā'* and not for writing is permitted, Ahf: 1/108].

4.6 The usage of a prescribed number of stones is *mustaḥab* and not *sunna mu^cakkada.*

To use three stones is *mustaḥab*, even though one may achieve cleanliness with less.

4.7 Method of performing *istinjā'*: if one's testicles are hanging one should wipe with the first stone from the front to the back and with the second from the back to the front and with the third from the front to the back [for fear of defiling one's testicles, Mf: p.89]. If the testicles are not hanging, then one should start from the back. A female should start from the front to the back for the fear of defiling her vagina.

4.8 Thereafter, one should wash the hand and using water wipe the soiled area with the inner side of one, two, or even three fingers if needed. A male will raise his middle finger over the rest when commencing the *istinjā'* [then after washing slightly, Mf: p.90] he will raise the ring finger [Z: and if need be then the small finger and then the index finger, Mf: p.90]. One should not suffice upon the use of one finger. A female should raise her ring and middle finger simultaneously from the outset for fear of being sexually aroused.

4.9 The utmost should be done in cleansing oneself until the foul smell has been eliminated, whilst thoroughly relaxing one's buttocks [Z: so as to clean what is in the passage to the best of one's ability, Mf: p.91], unless fasting. Upon completion one should wash the hand again. If fasting one should wipe oneself before standing.

4.10 It is unlawful to uncover one's *ᶜawra* (the private parts that need to be covered) for *istinjā'* in the presence of others. [Z: If one does, he will be regarded a *fāsiq*. The uncovering of one's *ᶜawra* in the presence of others is *ḥarām* (def: 1.5) and the perpetrator of a *ḥarām* act is regarded as a *fāsiq*, regardless of whether the *najāsa* has spread past the orifice or has exceeded the size of a *dirham*, Mf+t: p.32].

If the *najāsa* has spread past the orifice and covered an area more than that of a *dirham*, then with the availability of any substance that will remove the *najāsa*, ritual prayer is unlawful.

One should try to remove the *najāsa* without exposing one's *ᶜawra* in the presence of others.

It is *makrūh* (def: 1.6) to perform *istinjā'* with:

(1) a bone [because it is the food of the *jinns*, Mf: p.93];

(2) the food of a man or animal [Z: as this would be disrespectful to sustenance, Mf: p.93];

(3) baked bricks, pottery, charcoal;

(4) glass, gypsum [Z: because of the physical harm that it may cause, Mf: p.93];

(5) items of value, such as a piece of velvet or cotton;

(6) and the usage of the right hand without an excuse. [Z: The scholars are unanimous that it is *mustaḥab* to start with the right in all those things of reverence, such as *wuḍū'*, bathing, wearing clothes, shoes, socks, trousers, when entering the mosque, when performing *miswāk*, applying antimony, trimming the nails,

plucking the hair from the armpits, when shaving the head, performing the *salām* at the termination of the prayer, when departing from the lavatory, whilst drinking, performing *istilām* (kissing) of the *ḥajr al-aswad* (the black stone), when taking, giving and other similar tasks. It is *mustaḥab* to start from the left when performing those actions which are to the contrary, i.e. not revered, such as blowing the nose, performing *istinjā'*, when entering the lavatory or departing from the mosque, removing the *khufayn*, shoes, trousers or other garments, *al-Bināya*, 1/188].

4.11 *Adāb* (def: 1.3) of relieving oneself:

(1) One should enter the toilet leading with the left foot;

(2) before entering seek refuge in Allah from the rejected Satan. [Whilst in the open one should recite the supplication before uncovering oneself, *I*ᶜ*lā al-sunan* 1/451];

«[بِسْمِ اللهِ] اللَّهُمَّ إِنِّي أَعُوذُ بِكَ مِنَ الْخُبُثِ وَالْخَبَائِثِ»

*Allahumma innī a*ᶜ*udhu bika min al-khubuthi wal khabā'ith*

[O Allah I take refuge in You from demons, male and female];

(3) one should sit leaning upon the left foot;

(4) and not speak, except out of necessity.

It is *makrūh taḥrīm* (whilst relieving oneself) to have one's face or back towards the *Qibla*, even though one is in a building. [Z: It is also *makrūh* to hold a child to urinate towards the *Qibla*, Mf: p.95]. To urinate towards the sun or moon is *makrūh* [being two great signs (*āyas*) of Allah. However, this act is considered *makrūh tanzīh* rather than *makrūh taḥrīm* according to Ibn ᶜĀbidīn, Mf: p.95]; it is also *makrūh* to sit and urinate in the direction of the wind. [Z: The reason for this is that the wind may blow the urine back to the person, thus causing his clothes to be soiled and the Prophet (may Allah bless him and grant him peace) warned against this in a number of *aḥādīth*].

4. 12 It is *makrūh*:

(1) To urinate or defecate in water;

(2) under some shade; in a hole; on the path;

(3) under a fruit tree;

(4) or urinate standing without an excuse.

[Z: It is *makrūh* to enter the toilet wearing anything with the name of Allah, Mf: p.96. Abū Dā'ūd and Tirmidhī have related upon the authority of Anas (may Allah be pleased with him) that he said, "When the Messenger of Allah (may Allah bless him and grant him peace) would enter the lavatory he would remove his ring, "because engraved upon it was 'Muḥammad the Messenger of Allah.'" Ṭībī commenting upon this states, "In this there is a proof that it is *wājib* upon the one performing *istinjā'* to remove anything with the name of Allah upon it or His Messenger or anything from the Qur'ān. Ibn Ḥajr has stated, "that it can be derived from this that it is *mustaḥab* to remove anything which has a revered name upon it from the Names of Allah, the Prophets or Angels." Not to remove it would be deemed *makrūh* due to disrespect, Mf+t p.35].

One should leave the lavatory with one's right foot then recite "[O Lord] Your forgiveness. Praise be to Allah who rid me of the filth and gave me health."

غُفْرَانَكَ اَلْحَمْدُ لِلّٰهِ الَّذِىْ اَذْهَبَ عَنِّى الْاَذٰى وَعَافَانِىْ۔

Ghufarānak alḥamdulilla hilladhī adhhaba ᶜannīl adha-wa-ᶜāfānī

Wuḍū' (Ablution)

5.1 The reason for performing *wuḍū'* is to make lawful that which is otherwise unlawful without it, these are its benefits in this world. Whilst its benefits in the Hereafter is the attainment of rewards.

5.2 *Wuḍū'* consists of four *farḍ* (def: 1.1) acts:

(1) To wash the face from the point where the hairline usually begins to the bottom of the chin in length, and in breadth the portion between the two earlobes. [Z: The definition of washing (*ghasl*) is that at least a couple of drops should flow off the limbs, Lub: p.6];

(2) washing the arms up to and including the elbows;

(3) to wash the feet up to and including the ankle bones;

(4) and to wipe with a moist hand (*masḥ*) over a quarter of the head.

5.3 Conditions for *Wuḍū'* to be *Farḍ*

(a) Sanity;

(b) puberty;

(c) one must be a Muslim;

(d) to possess enough water [Z: to be able to wash the required limbs at least once, Mf: p.100];

(e) to be ritually impure [the performance of *wuḍū'* for one who is already in the state of *wuḍū'* is not necessary, Mf: p.100];

(f) to be free from menses and postnatal bleeding;

(g) and to have enough time. [Z: The obligation of *wuḍū'* is dropped if there is insufficient time to perform *wuḍū'* before the expiry of the *ṣalāh* time. However, this should not be understood to mean that prayer is permissible without *wuḍū'*. One will be required to make up the prayer later with *wuḍū'*].

5.4 **Conditions for the validity of *Wuḍū'***

(1) Pure water reaches the skin of those parts which are required to be washed;

(2) that one is free from those things which are incompatible with *wuḍū'*, such as menses, postnatal bleeding, factors perpetuating ritual impurity, [such as the intermittent drops of urine and the occurrence of that which invalidates *wuḍū'*, Mf: p.101];

(3) and the removal of that which prevents the water from reaching the skin, such as wax and fat. [The same applies of waterproof glue, paint, nail polish, and so forth on the nails or skin: if it prevents water from reaching *any part* of the nails or skin no matter how small, one's ablution or purificatory bath is not valid, *Reliance of the Traveller,* p.67].

5.5 It is incumbent to wash the visible part of a thick beard [through which the skin is not visible, Mf: p.101]. As for a sparse beard it is incumbent that the water reaches the skin. Whilst it is not necessary that water reaches the hair hanging from the periphery of the face, nor that water reaches the concealed part of the lips when the mouth is closed.

5.6 If the fingers are tightly held together, or a nail has grown so long that it has covered the finger tip, or there is something in the nail which prevents the water from reaching the finger tip, such as dough, then it will be incumbent [to remove the substance, Mf: p.102] and wash underneath. Substances such as dirt do not prevent the penetration of water.

5.7 It is incumbent that a tight ring be moved about. If washing the cracks in one's feet is harmful, then it will suffice to allow water to flow over the medicine applied to them.

5.8 One is not required to repeat the *masḥ* or washing of any limb from where the hair have been shaved, nor is one required to wash after cutting one's nails or trimming one's moustache.

Sunnas of _Wuḍū'_

5.9 There are eighteen *sunnas* (def: 1.3) of *wuḍū'*:

(1) Washing the hands including the wrists;

(2) the recitation of the *basmallah* (the formula, 'In the name of Allah the Most Compassionate the Most Merciful');

(3) to use the *miswāk* (tooth-stick) when commencing the *wuḍū'*, to use one's finger in the absence of the *miswāk*. [Z: Regarding toothbrushes two things have to be taken into consideration, firstly the *sunna* of cleansing one's mouth. Secondly, the usage of the *sunna siwāk* (the *sunna* instrument). Regarding the *sunna* of cleansing one's mouth in the absence of the *sunna* tooth-stick the jurists have stated that one may use a piece of cloth, tooth powder or even one's finger. As long as the bristles of the toothbrush are made of a pure substance the *sunna* of cleansing one's mouth will be fulfilled. However, the virtues mentioned will only be attained through using the *sunna* tooth-stick which is from the olive, salvadora or margosa tree. Similarly, using anything other than the *sunna* tooth-stick will

not equal the benefits gained for one's gums and teeth, *Dars-i-Tirmidhi,* 1/228].

[Z: the *sunna* method of using a *miswāk* is to perform vertical strokes upon the teeth, *Dars-i-Tirmidhi,* 1/225];

(4) to rinse the mouth thrice, even if it is with a single handful of water;

(5) to rinse the nose with three handfuls of water;

(6) if not fasting, to rinse thoroughly the mouth and nose;

(7) to saturate a thick beard by inserting a handful of water from underneath and then to comb it with the fingers upwards;

(8) to pass the wet fingers of one hand into the gaps between the fingers of the other hand, [Z: whilst with the toes one uses the little finger of the left hand beginning with the little toe of the right foot and finishes with the little toe of the left, Mf+t: p.46];

(9,10) to wash each limb thrice; to do the *masḥ* of the entire head once;

(11) and the *masḥ* of the ears, even though it may be with the leftover water from the *masḥ* of the head. [The *masḥ* of the outside of the ear should be done with the thumb and the inside of the ear with the index finger, Mf+t: p.47 (see: fig, 1)];

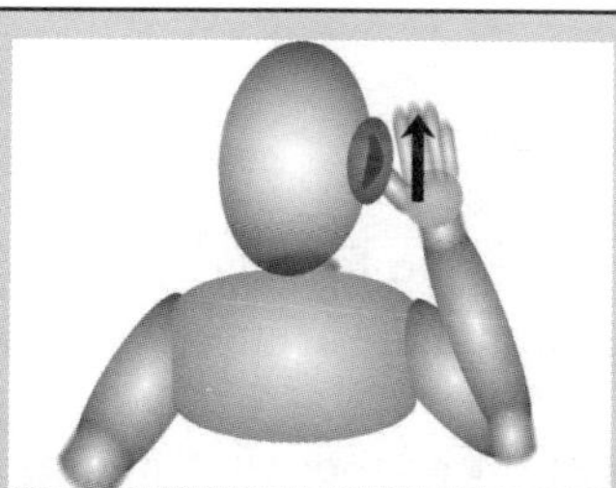

Fig. 1
Masḥ behind the ears

(12) to rub the limbs;

(13) to perform the actions of *wuḍū'* successively [which is to wash each limb before the former dries, Mf: p.109];

(14) to make an intention;

(15) to observe the order ordained by Allah in the Qur'ān;

(16) to start from the right;

(17) to commence the washing from the tips of the fingers and the performance of the *masḥ* of the head from the front;

(18) to wipe the nape and not the throat (see: fig, 2);

It is an opinion that the last four are *mustaḥab.*

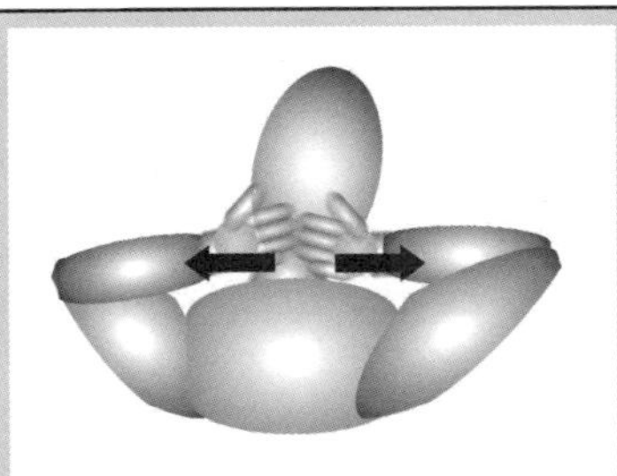

Fig. 2
Masḥ of the nape with the back of the hands.

Adāb* (def: 1.4) of *Wuḍū'

5.10 There are fourteen *adāb* of *wuḍū'*:

(1,2,3,4) To sit upon an elevated place; to face the *Qibla*; to take no assistance; and not to speak of mundane affairs;

(5) to combine between the intention of the heart and a verbal formula;

(6) to recite the transmitted supplications [from the Prophet (may Allah bless him and grant him peace), the Companions and their Successors, Mf: p.112];

(7,8,9) to recite the *basmallah* whilst washing or doing *masḥ* of each limb; to insert one's small finger into the canals of the ears; and to move a loose ring;

(10,11) to use the right hand in inserting the water into the mouth and nose; and to use the left hand to clean the nose;

(12) for other than a *ma^cdhūr* (def: 9.10) to perform *wuḍū'* upon the entry of the *ṣalāh* time;

13) to recite the two declarations of faith after completing the *wuḍū'*;

«أَشْهَدُ أَنْ لَا إِلَهَ إِلَّا اللهُ وَحْدَهُ لَا شَرِيكَ لَهُ، وَأَشْهَدُ أَنَّ مُحَمَّدًا عَبْدُهُ وَرَسُولُهُ

Ashhadu alla illāha ilallahu wa ashhadu anna Muḥammadan abdhū wa ar-rasulluhū

14) to drink the remainder of the water of *wuḍū'* standing and then to recite, "O Allah make me from the repenters and make me from those who attain purity."

«اللَّهُمَّ اجْعَلْنِي مِنَ التَّوَّابِينَ وَاجْعَلْنِي مِنَ الْمُتَطَهِّرِينَ»

Allahum maj'alnī minat tawwābīna wa j'alnī minal mutaṭ āhhirīn

Makrūh (def: 1.6) acts in *Wuḍū'*

5.11 The *makrūh* acts in *wuḍū* are six:

(1) Wasting water [Z: that is when one exceeds the *sunna* method, Mf+t: p.53];

(2) being miserly with it [Z: that is when one uses less than the *sunna* method, Mf+t: p.53];

(3) to splash one's face with water;

(4) to speak of mundane affairs;

(5) to seek the assistance of others without an excuse;

(6) and to do *masḥ* of the head thrice with new water.

Types of *Wuḍū'*

5.12 There are three types of *wuḍū'* :

(1) *Farḍ* (def: 1.1), upon one who wishes to perform a ritual prayer, even though it be *nawāfil* (supererogatory prayers), or the *janāza* (the congregational prayer over the deceased, the performance of which is *al-farḍ al-kifāya* (def: 1.8)), or for *sajda al-tilāwa* (prostration which becomes obligatory upon reciting certain verses of the Qur'ān), or to touch the Qur'ān, even a single verse;

(2) *wājib* (def: 1.1), for the circumambulation (*ṭawāf*) of the Holy Ka^{c}ba;

(3) and *mustaḥab* (def: 1.2);

(a) for one wishing to sleep in a ritually pure state;

(b) upon awaking;

(c) so that one can be continuously in the state of *wuḍū';*

(d) for the performance of *wuḍū'* for one who is already in the state of *wuḍū';*

(e) after backbiting, telling lies, carrying tales and any other sin;

(e) after the recitation of [foul, Mf: p.120] poetry;

(g) after laughing loudly outside *ṣalāh;*

(h) after bathing or carrying a dead body;

(i) for the time of each *ṣalāh;*

(j) before bathing from major ritual impurity;

(k) before eating, drinking and sleeping for the one in a state of major ritual impurity;

(l) before having sexual intercourse;

(m) upon becoming angry;

(n) for the recitation of the Qur'ān;

(o) the reading and transmitting of *aḥādīth*;

(p) for the studying of sacred knowledge. [Z: It is unlawful to touch books on Qur'anic exegesis without *wuḍū'* if the original Qur'anic text is more than the exegesis. If on the other hand the exegesis constitutes the greater part then it is lawful provided one does not put his hands directly on the Qur'anic verses, Ahf: 1/27];

(q) before performing the *adhān* (call to prayer), *iqāma* (call for commencement) and *khutba* (Friday sermon);

(r) when visiting the tomb of our master the Prophet (may Allah bless him and grant him peace);

(s) for staying at the plain of *ᶜArafa* (the name of a plain approximately thirteen miles to the east of Makkah);

(t) before pacing (*saᶜī*) between *al-Ṣaffa* and *al-Marwa* (two hillocks connected by a course adjoining *al-Masjid al-Ḥaram*);

(u) after eating camel meat;

(v) and to avoid the differences of the scholars by performing *wuḍū'* (after performing an act upon which they differ) such as touching a female.

[Z: An additional two categories which may be introduced are *makrūḥ* (def: 1.5) and *ḥarām* (def: 1.4), an example of the former, is to perform *wuḍū'* whilst still in the state of *wuḍū'* without having performed any such worship which necessitates *wuḍū'*. An example of the latter is to do *wuḍū'* whilst still in the state of *wuḍū'* with the water of an Islamic institute (*madarasa*) or *waqf* (endowment) water, Mf+t: p.45].

Things that Nullify the *Wuḍū'*

5.13 There are twelve things that nullify *wuḍū'*:

(1) Anything which exits from the front and back passage of the private parts, besides wind from the front passage:

(2) after giving birth even though no blood is visible;

(3) the flowing of impurity from anywhere else other than the front and back passage of the private parts, such as blood and puss.

(4) Vomiting a mouthful of food, water, blood clots or bile. The correct view on determining '*a mouthful* ' is that one is unable to close one's mouth except through difficulty.

Vomiting several times is regarded as vomiting once, if gathered, the summation would reach a mouthful provided that the cause for each vomit is the same.

(5) An equal amount or predominance of blood upon one's spit. [Z: If the spit is yellowish this would indicate to the predominance of the spit; whilst a reddish colour would indicate to the predominance of blood. This ruling applies when the emission of blood is from the gums. However, if it is from the head or chest, then however small the amount of blood, it shall annul the *wuḍū'* , ai: p.49];

(6) to sleep in such a way that one's buttocks are not firmly established upon the earth;

(7) or to sleep in such a way that one's buttocks rise off the floor before one awakes, even though one may not fall as a result of them rising.

[Z: The *ᶜilla* (reason) why *wuḍū'* breaks when one sleeps is not 'sleep' itself, but the possibility that as a result of sleeping one's limbs may have become so relaxed that they may have allowed wind to escape. This is why if one sleeps in a posture in which the limbs remain stiff, such as sleeping in *sajda* (prostration) or *rukūᶜ* (bowing) then one's *wuḍū'* will remain intact].

(8,9,10) Due to losing consciousness, or one's sanity and upon becoming drunk;

(11) loud laughter by a conscious adult in any ritual prayer consisting of *rukū*ᶜ (bowing) and *sujūd* (prostrating). [Z: Loud laughter (*qahqaha*) is when one standing in close proximity can hear the laughter. Laughter (*ḍiḥk*) which only the one laughing is able to hear will annul one's *ṣalāh* but not the *wuḍū'* and smiling (*tabassum*) would have no bearing on either, Mf: p125].

(12) Rubbing a vagina with an erect penis without any form of a barrier. [Z: If the barrier is thin such as a condom or a thin piece of clothing through which one can feel the sensation then this will annul the *wuḍū'*, ai: p.49].

Things that do not Nullify *Wuḍū'*

5.14 Things that do not nullify *wuḍū'* are ten:

(1) Blood which has not flowed from its wound; [If one wipes the blood from the head of the wound, such that if it was not wiped the impurity would spread, then the *wuḍū'* will be considered invalid, *Sharḥ fatḥ al-qadīr,* 1/39];

(2) the loss of a piece of flesh without any blood flowing;

(3) the exiting of a worm from one's wound, ear or nose;

(4,5) touching one's penis, [or vagina or anus, Mf: p.127]; or a female;

(6,7) vomit which is not a mouthful; or a mouthful or more but that of phlegm;

(8,9) the swaying of a sleeping person in such a way that it is possible that his buttocks may have lifted; or one whose buttocks are established upon the earth, even though he is leaning upon an object which, if removed, would cause him to fall;

10) the sleeping of one who is praying, even though it may be whilst performing *rukū* or *sujūd,* provided he maintains his posture according to the *sunna.* [If one's posture is no longer according to the *sunna,* then one's *wuḍū'* will be invalidated such as one's arms collapsing upon the rib area or the stomach collapsing upon the thighs in *sujūd,* ai: p.51].

Ghusl (Bathing)

Things that necessitate *Ghusl*

6.1 Things that necessitate *ghusl* are six:

(1) The emission of sperm which has departed from its origin [which is the loins, Mf: p.50], whilst one is in a state of sexual arousal provided this emission has taken place without intercourse. [Z: In the case of intercourse, mere penetration compels a bath there is no condition of emission].

[The departure of the semen from its place of origin without one being in the state of sexual arousal does not obligate *ghusl*, such as its emission upon picking up a heavy object, ai: p.53];

(2) the insertion of the head of the penis (circumcised portion) or a portion which is equivalent to the head if the penis is cut into the vagina or anus of a living person;

(3) one who awakens to find a thin liquid and his penis was not erect before sleeping [Z: if the penis was erect prior to sleeping it is a likelihood that the wetness is *madhī* (def: 6.2 (1)), ai: p.53];

(4) when recovering from intoxication or upon regaining consciousness one finds some wetness which one believes to be sperm;

(5) upon the stopping of menstruation;

(6) or postnatal bleeding.

Even though the aforementioned things may have occurred prior to embracing Islam.

It is *al-farḍ al-kifāya* (communal obligation (def: 1.8)) to bathe a dead person.

Things that do not necessitate *Ghusl*

6.2 Things that do not necessitate *ghusl* are eight:

(1,2) The emission of *madhī* [a thin, sticky, white fluid caused by amorous play or kissing] or *wadī* [a thick white cloudy liquid, which has no smell. It generally exits after one urinates and occasionally before];

(3) upon witnessing an erotic dream but awaking to find no wetness;

(4) to give birth without any visible trace of blood succeeding it;

(5) the insertion of a penis which is wrapped in such a cloth that prevents sexual arousal;

(6) after the administration of a medicine to a sick person by his anus;

(7) by inserting a finger or something similar into the front or back passage of the private parts;

(8) and penetrating a virgin in such a manner that she does not become deflowered provided one has not ejaculated. [Z: Her virginity remaining intact would ensure that the circumcisible parts did not meet in a way that would necessitate a purificatory bath, Mf: p.136].

[Z: *Ghusl* is not *farḍ* upon a woman who during postnatal bleeding, experiences a wet dream. A single purificatory bath will suffice for both the wet dream and postnatal bleeding upon the termination of the bleeding, Ahf 1/32].

The *Farā'iḍ* (sing: *Farḍ* (def: 1.1)) of *Ghusl*

6.3 There are eleven *farā'iḍ* of *ghusl*:

(1,2,3) To rinse the mouth and nose and wash the entire body;

(4,5,6) to clean the inner part of the circumcisable part provided it can be opened without any difficulty; to wash the inner part of the navel; to wash the inside of a hole which has not sealed;

(7) to undo the plaits of a man's hair, even if water reaches the roots. A female is exempt from undoing her plaits as long as the water reaches the roots; [If a woman's hair is so compact that it prevents the water penetrating to the roots then it is obligatory to open the plaits, Mf: p.138];

(8,9,10) to ensure that water reaches to the skin underneath the beard, moustache and eyebrows;

(11) and to ensure that water reaches the external part of the vagina, [Z: that area that is generally regarded necessary to wash in *istinjā'*, ai: p.56].

The *Sunnas* of *Ghusl*

6.4 The *sunnas* of *ghusl* are twelve:

(1) To begin with; 'In the Name of Allah the Most Beneficent, The Most Merciful';

(2) to make an intention;

(3) to wash the hands up to and including the wrists;

(4) to wash away the *najāsa* even though it be on separate places, [Z: this should be done before commencing the bath, Mf: p.140];

(5) to wash the sexual organs;

(6) to perform *wuḍū'* as one does for *ṣalāh,* to wash thrice and to do *masḥ* of the head;

(7) to delay the washing of the feet if one is standing in a place where water accumulates;

(8) to pour water over the entire body thrice, or by plunging into running water or anything of similar legal status [such as a large quantity of water (def: 2.2 (4))], if after plunging in such water one remains therein a while the *sunna* will also be fulfilled. [To wash thrice is *sunna* so as to ensure that water reaches all the required parts. By remaining under the water the *sunna* of making the water reach all parts will be fulfilled, ai: p.59. Provided that it is performed after rinsing the mouth and nose, otherwise one is still obliged to rinse the mouth and nose, and its omission would lead to the invalidity of the purificatory bath, ai: p.58];

(9,10) one should begin by pouring water over one's head, then the right shoulder thereafter the left;

(11) to rub the body;

(12) and to be continuous in washing [Z: one should not wait so long that the previously washed limbs become dry, ai: p.58].

The *Adāb* (def: 1.4) and *Makrūh* (def: 1.6) things in *Ghusl*

6.5 The *adāb* are the same as that of *wuḍū'* (see: 5.10), except that one should not face the *Qibla*, because generally one is in a naked state.

6.6 That which is *makrūh* in *wuḍū'* (see: 5.11) is *makrūh* in *ghusl.*

[Z: If the bathroom is filthy, then one should enter like one does the toilet with the left foot leading. As mentioned it is *sunna* to recite the *basmallah* before the *ghusl,* however in a filthy bathroom the recitation will occur before entering the bathroom and the supplication (*du*ᶜ*a*) for after the *wuḍū'* will be recited upon leaving. In a clean bathroom which has no toilet, the *basmallah* may be recited before removing one's clothing, Ahf: 1/37].

Occasions when *Ghusl* is *Sunna*

6.7 There are four occasions when *ghusl* is *sunna*:

For the (i) *jumu*ᶜ*a*, (ii) ᶜ*id* prayers, (iii) for wearing the *iḥrām* (the state of consecration that pilgrims enter for *ḥajj* and ᶜ*umra*), (iv) and after the zenith (*zawāl*) at the ᶜ*Arafa* (def: 5.12 (r)) for one performing *ḥajj* .

Occasions when *Ghusl* is *Mustaḥab*

6.8 There are sixteen occasions when *ghusl* is *mustaḥab*;

(1) For one embracing Islām while free from major ritual impurity [if the person is in the state of major ritual impurity then *ghusl* is *farḍ,* ai: p.61];

(2) one who has become mature through age [the prescribed age is fifteen for a boy or girl, Mf: p.146];

(3) upon regaining one's sanity [or recovering from a drunken state or upon regaining consciousness, Mf: p.146];

(4) after cupping;

(5) after bathing a dead body;

(6) for the night of immunity (*laylat al-barā*);

(7) for the one who observes the night of decree *(laylat al-qadr*);

(8) for entering into Madina, the city of our master Muḥammad (may Allah bless him and grant him peace);

(9) for the morning stay at *Muzdalifa* upon the day of immolation;

(10) upon entering into Makkah for the *ṭawāf al-ziyāra* [Z: due to the occurrence of *ṭawāf al-ziyāra, ramya al-jimār* and the stay at *Muzdalifa* all on one day, one bath with the intention of all three will suffice, Mf+t: p.79];

(11,12,13) for the eclipse of the sun, of the moon and seeking rain prayers;

(14,15,16) for the prayer of fear (*ṣalāh al-khawf*) and due to darkness [during the day, Mf: p.147] or a strong wind.

[Z: It is also *mustaḥab* to perform *ghusl* for one returning from a journey or one wanting to repent, one about to be killed, upon recovery from irregular vaginal bleeding and for the one who has *najāsa* (def: 10.1) upon his body but is unsure exactly where it is, Mf: p.147]

Other relevant issues:

6.9 [Z: A narration related by Imām Muslim, delineates the requirement to trim the moustache, nails, pluck the hair from the armpits and shave the pubic hairs within the period of forty days. However, the prescription of forty days is to illustrate the maximum period one should forgo without performing the aforementioned acts and not necessarily the most preferable period. The Prophet (may Allah bless him and grant him peace) would trim his nails and moustache every Friday (before the *jumu*[c]*a* prayer) he would shave around his private parts after every twenty days and pluck the hair from his armpits every forty days.

It must be borne in mind that the purpose of shaving is to remove any hair that may impede one from attaining thorough cleanliness, therefore, no minimum period can be appointed given that the rate as to which hair grow differ from person to person. The recommended method would be that one shave before the hair grow so long that they become an obstacle in attaining cleanliness provided this is performed within the period of forty days. To exceed forty days is *makrūh, Kawkab al-durrī* [c]*ala jāmi*[c] *al-tirmidhī*, 3/401.

One should shave the hair directly around or on the penis, testicles and vagina and that what is around the rear passage, *Sharḥ ṣaḥīḥ muslim*, 3/150].

Tayammum (Dry Ablution)

7.1 There are eight conditions for its validity:

(1) Intention is a mental resolve upon the action. The time for the intention is when one places his hands upon the substance with which one intends to do *tayammum.* There are three conditions for the validity of the intention (i) that one should be a Muslim; (ii) possess the faculty whereby one can elicit meanings; (iii) and the knowledge of what one is intending, [if one recites the intention in Arabic without understanding the meaning such an intention is not valid, ai: p.64].

One of three things are a condition for one's intention of *tayammum* to suffice for performing *ṣalāh* with it: (i) to remove ritual impurity; (ii) that one becomes legally fit for *ṣalāh*; (iii) and to be legally fit for a specific worship which is not valid without legal purity. If whilst performing *tayammum* one has intended nothing more than *tayammum*, then with such a *tayammum* one shall not be permitted to perform *ṣalāh.* Similarly, when one has performed *tayammum* for the recitation of the Qur'ān [Z: this applies to mere recitation without touching the Qur'an], it is unlawful to perform *ṣalāh* with such a *tayammum* [because mere recitation does not necessitate legal purity], unless one was in the state of major ritual impurity.

(2) One who has a legitimate excuse to perform *tayammum*, such as: being a mile from water, though in a city, illness or severe cold or one who fears that performing *wuḍū'* may result in the loss of a limb or one may become ill. Similarly, for the fear of an enemy, [such as a human or anything else, this fear maybe for one's life, property or something entrusted to one, Mf: p.152], or thirst, or when the water is needed for baking bread, this does not apply to cooking a curry, in the absence of a necessary instrument for obtaining the water, [such as a rope or bucket, Mf: p.153], upon the fear of missing the *janāza* (def:

5.12 (1)) or *ᶜīd* prayers, for the one whose *wuḍū'* breaks whilst performing the *janāza* or *ᶜīd* prayers [Z: and fears that by the time he performs *wuḍū'* the congregational prayer will have finished], even though he may have begun his *ṣalāh* with the Imām and then his *wuḍū'* broke. This ruling does not extend to the one who fears that he will miss the *jumuᶜa* prayer, or the prayer time will expire for anyone of the five daily prayers.

(3) *Tayammum* should be performed with a pure earthly substance, such as soil, stone and sand and not upon wood, silver and gold. [It is unlawful to do *tayammum* with anything which becomes ash after being burnt, or with that which melts like gold and silver, ai: p.64].

(4) That all the required area be covered [which is the face, hands and arms up to and including the elbows, Mf: p.155] with the wiping.

(5) One should perform the wiping with the entire hand or the greater part of it; it shall not suffice to wipe with two fingers, even though by repeatedly wiping one covers the required area. For the wiping of the head during *wuḍū'* this repeated action will suffice.

(6) To gently strike one's palms on the earth twice, though these strikes maybe in one place. If one rubs the soil already upon one's body with the intention of *tayammum* this will substitute for the two strokes.

(7) The termination of those things which are incompatible with *tayammum*, such as menstruation, postnatal bleeding or factors perpetuating ritual impurity.

(8) The removal of those things which prevent *masḥ* such as wax and fat.

7.2 The reasons for *tayammum* and the conditions for it being *farḍ* are the same as those for *wuḍū'* (see: 5.3).

There are Two Integrals of *Tayammum:*

7.3 The wiping of the face and arms up to and including the elbows.

The *Sunnas* of *Tayammum*

7.4 There are seven *sunnas* of *tayammum*

(1,2,3) The recitation of the *basmallah* (def: 5.9 (2)) before commencement; the observance of the order; [as illustrated by the Prophet (may Allah bless him and grant him peace), Mf: p.158]; to perform the *tayammum* uninterruptedly;

(4,5,6,7) to move the hands forwards and backwards when placed upon the soil; to shake off the soil; and to keep the fingers wide open [whilst striking the soil, Mf: p.158].

7.5 It is *mustaḥab* to delay the *tayammum* for the one who anticipates that he will attain water before the expiry of the *ṣalāh* time. And obligatory for the one who has been promised water [and the promise is made by one who has water within the radius of a mile, ai: p.70], even though one may fear that the *ṣalāh* time may expire.

7.6 It is obligatory to delay the prayer for one [who is naked Mf: p.159] and has been promised clothing. It is also obligatory for one who has been promised an instrument for attaining water [such as a rope or bucket, Mf: p.159], however, this is when one does not fear the expiry of the *ṣalāh* time.

7.7 It is incumbent to seek water from one possessing some, if one is in a place where people are generally not miserly with it. If it cannot be acquired without paying the average price, then its purchase is obligatory unless one has only enough wealth for his basic requirements.

7.8 It is permissible to perform any number of *farā'id* (obligatory prayers) and *nawāfil* (supererogatory prayers) with a single *tayammum.* It is also permissible to perform the *tayammum* before the admittance of the time of *ṣalāh.*

7.9 If half or more of the body is wounded then one may perform *tayammum*; [Z: in *wuḍū'* the four limbs which are *farḍ* (see: 5.2) will have to be taken into consideration, whilst for a purificatory bath it is the entire body]. If, however, the greater part is free from wounds then one should wash the unwounded limbs and wipe over the wounded ones. It is not permitted to combine between washing and *tayammum.*

Those things which Nullify *Tayammum*

7.10 *Tayammum* is nullified by those things which nullify *wuḍū'* and also with the availability of sufficient water to perform *wuḍū'* with.

7.11 When he whose hands and feet have been amputated has a wound upon his face, then he may pray without purity (*ṭahāra*) and will not be obliged to repeat the prayer.

Masḥ over the *Khufayn* (sing: *khuf*)

8.1 It is lawful for both men and women to do *masḥ* over the *khufayn* for minor ritual impurity. Even if the *khufayn* are made of a thick substance other than leather, irrespective of whether the soles are of leather or not.

[Z: Footwear, which is made of wool or cotton is known as *jawrab.* That which has a leather sole and upper is known as *mujallad*, if only the sole is made of leather then it is known as *munᶜal.* Footwear, which is made of entirely leather, is known as *khuf.* To do *masḥ* is lawful upon all the aforementioned. However, if the *jawrab* is neither *mujallad* nor *munᶜal* and is made of a thin substance then it is unlawful to do *masḥ* upon it, *Dars-i-Tirmidhī,* 1/335].

Conditions for the Permissibility of *Masḥ* over the *Khufayn*:

8.2 are seven:

(1) That they be worn after washing the feet, even though this be before completing the *wuḍū'*, as long as the *wuḍū'* is completed before the *occurrence of anything* that invalidates the *wuḍū'*;

(2) the *khuf* must cover [Z: the foot up to and including] the ankle;

(3) it should be possible to walk continuously in the *khufayn.* It is unlawful to do *masḥ* over *khufayn* made of glass, wood or metal;

(4) each *khuf* must be free from any tear equivalent in size to the three smallest toes. [Z: If the multiple tears from both *khufs*

are amassed and the summation is equivalent to three toes this will not invalidate the *masḥ,* ai: p.75];

(5,6) the *khufayn* should cling to the feet without being tied; and prevent water from reaching the skin;

(7) at least the equivalent of three of the smallest fingers of the hand from the front of the foot should exist, if this amount is absent then it is unlawful to do *masḥ* over the *khuf*, even though the heel of the foot exists.

Duration of *Masḥ* over the *Khufayn:*

8.3 A resident, i.e. a non traveller, is permitted to do *masḥ* for a day and night [twenty four hours], while the duration for a traveller is three days and nights [seventy two hours]. The commencement of this period is from when *one becomes ritually impure* after wearing the *khufayn.*

[Z: If one performs *wuḍū'* at twelve and wears his *khufayn* and at three breaks his *wuḍū'* then the duration of *masḥ* over the *khufayn* will commence from three].

If a resident performs *masḥ* and then decides to travel before the expiry of his period he may complete the duration allowed to a traveller. If a traveller who has wiped over his *khufayn* becomes a resident after a day and night has lapsed, then he is obliged to remove his *khufayn.* In the event of becoming a resident within a day and night, he may complete the period prescribed for a resident.

The portion upon which it is *Farḍ* to do *Masḥ* over the *Khufayn*:

8.4 It is *farḍ* to do *masḥ* upon a portion equivalent to the three smallest fingers of the hand over the top frontal part of each *khuf,* and the *sunna* is to start from the tips of the toes with spread fingers up until the shin [see fig: 3].

[Z: One wishing to wear the *khuf* over a bandaged foot should first do *masḥ* over the bandage and then wear the *khuf,* ai: p.75].

[The *masḥ* must be performed over the area of the *khuf* wherein the foot lies. The *masḥ* of one wearing a very long or wide *khuf,* if performed over that area beneath which there is no foot, shall not suffice, ai: p.77].

Fig. 3
Masḥ upon the *khuf*

Things that Nullify *Masḥ* over the *Khufayn*:

8.5 Things that nullify *masḥ* over the *khufayn* are four:

(1) Everything that nullifies *wuḍū',* nullifies the *masḥ* over the *khufayn*;

(2) the removal of the *khuf*, this will also be effected by the greater part of the foot coming out of the leg of the *khuf* ;

(3) by water reaching into the greater portion of any one of the two feet that are in the *khufayn* ;

(4) the expiry of the prescribed time [see 8.3 for prescribed periods for traveller and resident], provided one does not fear that one's feet will perish due to cold conditions. [If one has such a fear, then one is permitted to do *masḥ* until one's conscience is satisfied, Mf: p.170].

In the case of the latter three (2-4), it will suffice to just wash the feet [one is not required to repeat *wuḍū'* if already in the state of *wuḍū'*, Mf: p.170].

8.6 It is unlawful to do *masḥ* over a turban, hat, veil or gloves.

8.7 If one has had blood drawn, been wounded or having broken a limb has tied a bandage or fixed a splint upon the affected area, and due to the severity of the injury is unable to wash the affected limb or do *masḥ* upon it directly, then it is obligatory to do *masḥ* upon the greater part of the splint or bandage.

8.8 It will suffice to do *masḥ* upon the skin visible between the rolls of the bandage.

Masḥ similar to washing has no time limit for its validity.

It is not a condition that the bandage be tied in a state of purity.

To do *masḥ* upon the bandaged foot whilst washing the other foot is permissible.

8.9 The bandage falling off before convalescence does not invalidate the *masḥ* [Z: and there is no compulsion to repeat the *masḥ* as long as one is in the state of *wuḍū'* , ai: p.79].

8.10 It is permissible to replace one bandage with another without it being necessary to repeat the *masḥ,* nevertheless, repetition is preferred.

8.11 If due to an inflammation of the eyes one is ordered by an [expert, Muslim doctor, Mf: p.173] not to wash his eyes, or one's nail has broken and he has applied some medicine to it, the removal of which is harmful then *masḥ* is permissible. If, however, *masḥ* itself is harmful then one is permitted to omit the *masḥ.*

There is no obligation to make an intention, [Z: unlike there is for *tayammum*], for performing *masḥ* upon the *khufayn*, a splint or the head.

Menstruation, Postnatal Bleeding and Irregular Vaginal Bleeding

Menstruation, postnatal bleeding and irregular vaginal bleeding all flow from the vagina:

9.1 *Ḥayḍ* (menstruation): Blood, which the womb of a mature female excretes, accompanied by no illness, pregnancy, and that she is not post-menopausal. Its minimum duration is three days, the average being five days, and the maximum being ten days.

9.2 *Nifās* (Postnatal bleeding): The blood following the birth of a child. Its maximum duration is forty days and there is no fixed minimum period.

9.3 *Istiḥāḍa* (Irregular vaginal bleeding): Blood which is seen for less than three days, or more than ten days during menstruation, or more than forty days following childbirth.

9.4 The duration of the *ṭuhr* (interval of purity between two menstruations), the minimum duration of cleanliness between two menstruations is fifteen days. There is no maximum duration.

Prohibitions due to Menstruation and Postnatal Bleeding

9.5 There are eight prohibitions:

(1,2,3,4) *Ṣalāh*, fasting, the recitation of even a single verse from the Qur'an [Z: to recite less than a verse without the intention of reciting the Qur'an is lawful, such as reciting *al-hamudu lillah* with the intention of gratitude or the recitation of the *basmallah* before eating, Lub: p.43], touching the Qur'an without a covering. [Z: The covering should be a third item such as a case or bag which is not physically attached to the

Qur'an, nor physically attached to the one wanting to touch the Qur'an such as his sleeve, *Sharḥ al-hidaya li imām [c]Abd al-Ḥai al-Lucknawī*, 1/212];

(5,6) entering the mosque, circumambulation of the Holy *Ka[c]ba*;

(7) intercourse;

(8) and sexual enjoyment of any part of the body from beneath the navel to beneath the knees.

Method of Becoming Pure

9.6 When the blood ceases on the longest duration fixed for menstruation [see: 9.1 for duration] or postnatal bleeding [see: 9.2 for duration], intercourse is permitted without a purificatory bath. However, if the bleeding ceases before the longest duration such has its termination on her general habit, then sexual intercourse is unlawful unless she performs a purificatory bath. [Z: If unable to do so for a legitimate reason then she performs Mf: p.180] *tayammum* and prays or a prayer time expires upon her. This is because upon the cessation of the blood, she had enough time to take a purificatory bath and recite the opening *Allāhu akbar* or more, but she did not bathe or perform *tayammum* until the time for the prayer had elapsed.

[Z: If the bleeding ceases at the time of the mid-morning prayer and she does not perform a purificatory bath or *tayammum*, then intercourse is unlawful until the time of the *zuhr* prayer expires, Mf+t: p.97].

9.7 A menstruating woman or one who has experienced child birth will make up the missed fasts by observing them at a later date when she is clean, but her missed prayers need not be made up.

9.8 There are five acts that become unlawful when one is in a state of *janāba* (major ritual impurity): (1) *Ṣalāh*, (2) recitation of even a verse of the Qur'ān, [Z: it is *makrūh* to recite the Qur'ān in a place of impurity such as a lavatory, abattoir and similar places, though it is lawful to recite the Qur'ān loudly in a clean bathroom provided there is no one present whose *ᶜawra* (def: 4.10) is exposed, otherwise recitation under one's breath is permitted, Mf+t: p.94], (3) to touch the Qur'ān without a covering, (4) to enter into a mosque (5) and the circumambulation of the Holy *Kaᶜba*.

9.9 There are three unlawful acts for a *muḥdith* (one in minor ritual impurity): (1) *Salāh*, (2) circumambulation of the Holy *Kaᶜba* (3) and the touching of the Qur'ān without a cover.

[Z: A woman whose normal habit of menstruation is five days, but occasionally after bathing and praying she experiences the reoccurrence of her bleeding. In such a case upon the fifth day when the bleeding stops she shall delay her bath to the end of the prayer time then take a bath and pray. Thereafter, if the bleeding resumes she shall abandon her prayers, Ahf: 1/68].

[Z: A woman whose normal cycle of menstruation is five days, but happens to terminate upon the fourth, will be required to fast and pray, and it will be incumbent upon her to delay the prayer to the end of the *mustaḥab* time. Sexual intercourse is unlawful until she completes her general habit of five days, Ahf: 1/68].

[Z: Bleeding that succeeds a miscarriage which has occurred upon four months or after into the pregnancy will be regarded as postnatal bleeding.

If the miscarriage occurred within four months of the pregnancy then it will be regarded as menstruation, provided the bleeding exceeds three days. Anything less than three days will be regarded as irregular vaginal bleeding.

If four months have not lapsed and one mistakenly takes the bleeding after the miscarriage to be postnatal bleeding and as a result abandoned prayer, these prayers will have to be made up, Ahf: 1/72].

Laws of Irregular Vaginal Bleeding and Others of Similar Standing

9.10 The legal ruling regarding the blood of irregular vaginal bleeding is the same as that of perpetual nasal haemorrhage and as such does not prevent the performance of *ṣalāh*, fasting or sexual intercourse. A woman suffering from irregular vaginal bleeding or one who has an ᶜ*udhr* (chronic annulment of *wuḍū')* such as being unable to stop intermittent drops of urine, or one whose bowels have become loose, should perform *wuḍū'* at the time of every *farḍ* prayer and pray with that *wuḍū'* as many *farḍ* or *nawāfil* as one wishes. [Z: *Farḍ* prayer refers to the prescribed prayer of that particular time or any other prayers which maybe *farḍ* to make up, Mf: p.183].

The ablution of one suffering from chronic annulment of *wuḍū'* (ᶜ*udhr*) becomes void only with the expiry of the prayer time [or the occurrence of that which invalidates the *wuḍū'* other than the present ᶜ*udhr*, Mf: p.183].

9.11 One is only considered a *ma*ᶜ*dhūr* (one suffering from chronic annulment of *wuḍū'*) when the ᶜ*udhr* remains intact for the full duration of a *farḍ* prayer in a way that it does not even cease for a time in which *wuḍū'* and *ṣalāh* can be performed.

9.12 The condition for the continuation of an ᶜ*udhr* is that once established (see: 9.10 for how it is established) it should re-occur during every prayer time at least once. The ᶜ*udhr* is nullified when a complete time of a *farḍ* prayer lapses in which the ᶜ*udhr* is absent.

[Z: It is incumbent for one suffering from chronic annulment of *wuḍū'* to change his clothing if they are continuously becoming impure. This is provided that after changing his clothes he can complete his prayer before they become soiled again. However, if this is not possible then the obligation to change them or wash them is lifted, Ahf: 1/75].

[For a hospital patient who is sure that his clothing is impure or has a doubt regarding their purity and due to his illness experiences difficulty in changing them, then he is permitted to pray in his soiled clothing, Ahf: 1/75].

9.13 [Z: If a woman who is suffering from irregular vaginal bleeding forgets her normal menstruation cycle by forgetting the number of days, but is able to recall that it occurs each month, then she shall abandon her prayer for three days from the first day when menstruation normally occurs. Regarding these three days she can be sure that they are *ḥayḍ*; for the following seven days she shall perform a bath for each *ṣalāh*, because of the uncertainty whether it is *istiḥāḍa* (def: 9.3) or *ḥayḍ* (def: 9.1). For the following twenty days she shall perform *wuḍū'* for each prayer, and this can be regarded as *ṭuhr* (def: 9.4). It is lawful for her in the period of *ṭuhr* to indulge in a conjugal relationship.

If the number of days is recalled (for example three), but in which part of the month they occurred is forgotten, then she shall pray for three days from the beginning of the month with a fresh *wuḍū'* for each prayer because of the uncertainty of whether she is in menstruation or *ṭuhr.* For the following twenty seven days she shall bathe for each prayer because of the possibility that she may have finished her *ḥayḍ* at any hour, Mf+t: p.93].

9.14 [Z: When the blood of a woman with a set habit exceeds the maximum period of ten days, then her set habit will be regarded as her menses and anything exceeding it as irregular vaginal bleeding. All the prayers that she abandoned after the duration of her set habit will have to be made up Lub: p.45. The same principal is extended to a woman who has a set habit in her postnatal bleeding, Lub: p.47].

Najāsa and the Method of Purification from it:

10.1 [Z: *Najāsa* is that which is defined unclean according to *sharī*[c]*a*].

10.2 There are two types of *najāsa*: strong (*ghalīza*) and light (*khafīfa*).

Examples of the strong *najāsa* are wine, flowing blood, the flesh of a dead animal and its hide, the urine of those animals whose flesh is unlawful for consumption, the excreta of a dog and of a predatory animal and its saliva, the droppings of a hen, duck or goose and also all those things which come out of a human body and nullify one's *wuḍū'* [such as flowing blood, semen, *madhī* (def: 6.2), *wadī* (def: 6.2), irregular vaginal bleeding (def: 9.3), menses, postnatal blood and a mouthful of vomit (def: 5.13 (4)), Mf: p.187. Vomit that is less than a mouthful, or blood that does not flow is considered pure, Mf+t: p.103].

10.3 Examples of light *najāsa* are: the urine of a horse, and of those animals whose flesh is lawful for consumption and the droppings of birds whose flesh is unlawful for consumption.

What can be overlooked from *najāsa:*

10.4 What is equal to the area of a *dirham* (def: 4.3) from *najāsa ghalīza* (strong filth) [If the amount reaches a *dirham* then it is *makrūh taḥrīm* to pray in such clothing, if it is less than a *dirham* then it is *makrūh tanzīh,* Mf+t: p.104]. What covers less than a quarter of a cloth or the body from *najāsa ḳhafīfa* (light filth) is overlooked. Splashes of urine that are equal in size to the heads of needles are also overlooked.

10.5 If a bed or soil which is afflicted by *najāsa* becomes wet due to the sweat of a sleeping person, or due to wet feet, and thereafter traces of *najāsa* appear upon one's body or feet then one's body or feet will be classed as impure. If there is no trace they will not be considered impure. Similarly, a dry pure cloth does not become impure when wrapped in a wet impure cloth which does not drip if wrung.

10.6 A wet cloth does not become impure when spread upon impure dry earth, which becomes moist through the wetness of the cloth. Nor does a cloth become impure after being afflicted by a wind which has blown over some *najāsa*, unless traces of the *najāsa* are visible in the cloth.

10.7 An object which has on it visible *najāsa* [that remains visible after drying, Mf+t: p.106], will become pure by the removal of the *najāsa*. This washing need only be performed once according to the soundest opinion. If it is difficult to remove the *najāsa*, then there is no harm if traces remain.

10.8 An object, that has on it invisible *najāsa* [which can no longer be seen upon drying, Mf+t: p.106], should be washed thrice and wrung after each washing. [Z: On the third time, one should wring it so thoroughly that all water ceases to drip. If the cloth is thin or of a delicate nature, then one is not required to exert one's total strength, Mf+t: p.107].

Najāsa is removed from a cloth or body by water or any liquid that removes *najāsa* such as vinegar or rose water.

10.9 *Khufayn* and the like become pure when wiped [with earth or soil, Mf: p194], provided the *najāsa* is solid, even though it may still be wet. A sword or similar items may be purified by wiping the *najāsa* away [with soil or a cloth, Mf: p.194].

10.10 When the traces of *najāsa* have disappeared from the earth and the earth has dried, then *ṣalāh* is permissible upon it, while *tayammum* is not. By the earth drying, what is upon it also becomes pure, such as a tree and standing grass.

[Z: A impure cloth, if washed under a flowing tap, is not required to be washed or wrung thrice, provided that the water used is equivalent to what would be generally used if it was washed thrice, Ahf: p.97].

10.11 *Najāsa* becomes pure when it is molecularly transformed into something else, like turning into salt or upon being burnt [Z: and becoming pure ashes, because its true nature has changed. An example is grape juice which has changed into wine, thus becoming impure, and then changed into vinegar, becoming pure again, Mf: p.196].

10.12 A cloth or body can be purified by scraping dry semen off, whilst purity from wet sperm is only attained by washing.

***Najāsa* (Impurity) is of two types**

Najāsa ghalīza (strong impurity) such as wine, flowing blood saliva of a predatory animal etc.

Najāsa khafīfa (light impurity) such as the urine of those animals whose flesh is lawful for consumption etc.

What is less than or equal in size to a *dirham* of *najāsa ghalīza* is overlooked.

What is less in area than a quarter of a cloth or of the body of *najāsa khafīfa* is overlooked.

An object that has visible *najāsa* on it will become pure by the removal of the *najāsa.*

An object, that has an invisible *najāsa* on it must be washed thrice and wrung out after each wash.

Khuf and the like become pure when wiped with earth or soil, provided the *najāsa* is visible.

A sword and the like can be purified by wiping the *najāsa* away with soil or a cloth.

Tanning the Hide

11.1 The hide of a dead animal is purified by tanning either *ḥaqīqīya,* such as using the pods of a sant tree, or *ḥukmīya* such as cleansing the hide with soil or by leaving it in the sun to dry. The hide of a swine or human cannot be used even after tanning.

11.2 Slaughtering in accordance with the *Sharī^{c}a* purifies the hides of those animals whose meat is unlawful for consumption, whilst their meat remains unlawful.

11.3 Those parts through which blood does not flow do not become impure by death, such as the hair, cut feathers, horns and hoofs, as long as there is no fat on them. The nerve is impure according to the soundest opinion. The musk bag is pure like musk itself and its consumption is lawful. Civet is pure and it is lawful for onc to apply its fragrance and to perform *ṣalāh* with it.

Glossary

adāb (sing: **adab**): that which the Prophet did once or twice throughout his life.

ᶜArafa the name of a plain about thirteen miles to the east-southeast of Makkah.

'awra the private parts that must be covered.

dirham A silver coin about the size of a British fifty pence piece.

diḥk laughter.

farḍ obligation (for more detail see 1.1).

al-farḍ al-kifāya: communal obligation (for more detail see 1.7).

fāsiq the one who flagrantly transgresses the laws of Allah.

ghusl a bath, often refers to a purificatory bath.

ḥarām forbidden unlawful.

hayḍ menstruation.

istiḥāḍa irregular vaginal bleeding.

istilām kissing of the Black Stone.

Jinns genie.

Laylat al-Barā Night of Immunity, occurrence of which takes place upon the fifteenth of Shabān.

Laylat al-Qadr *It is the most virtuous night of the year. Allah says regarding it the Qur'an, 'We have revealed it (the Qur'an) on the night of qadr. What will tell what the night of power is? It is better than a thousand years.'*

Scholars have differed regarding when this night occurs. However, the majority view is that it occurs on one of the odd nights in the last ten days of Ramadan.

makrūh : According to the Ḥanafī's is a command for abstinence from something established by a speculative proof. It is divided into two categories, namely, *makrūh tahrīm* and *makrūḥ tanzīh* The latter is closer to *ḥarām* and can also be defined as being in diametrical opposition to a *wājib. Makrūh tanzih* is closer to *mubāḥ* and in diametrical opposition to a *mustaḥab.*

masḥ to wipe, sometimes referring to wiping with wet hands and at others with dry hands.

miswāk tooth-stick.

mubāḥ permissible, a *mubāḥ* act is neither rewarded nor punished.

mustaḥab that which the Prophet (may Allah bless him and grant him peace) did occasionally.

muṭlaq absolute, pure.

Muzdalifa a place near Makka where the pilgrims spend the night on their return from ᶜ*Arafa.*

najāsa filth, actual or ritual.

nawāfil supererogatory worship.

nifās postnatal bleeding.

qahqaha loud laughter.

ramya al-jimār the casting of the stones at Mina.
al-Ṣaffa and *al-Marwa*: two hillocks connected by a course adjoining *al-masjid al-ḥarām*.

sajda al-tilāwa an obligatory prostration for the recitation of certain verses of the Holy Qur'an.

sharīᶜa the embodiment of Islāmic laws.

sujūḍ prostration.

su'r leftovers.

sunna literally, means a clear path or beaten track, refers to whatever the Prophet (may Allah bless him and grant him peace) said, did, agreed to or condemned. The *sunna* is a source of the *Sharīᶜa* and a legal proof next to the Qur'ān. As a source of the *Sharīᶜa.* The *sunna* may corroborate a ruling which originates in the Qur'ān. Secondly, the *sunna* may consist of an explanation or clarification of the Qur'ān. Thirdly, the *sunna* may also consist of rulings on which the Qur'ān is silent.

tabassum smile.

tawāf al-ziyārah the obligatory circumambulation of the Holy Kaᶜba after throwing the pebbles at the *jamarāt.* It is also known *ṭawāf al-ifāḍa.*

tayammum dry Ablution.

ṭuhr interval of purity between two menstruations.

'udhr literally means excuse, technically, in the context of our work, chronic annulment of *wuḍū'*.

wadī a thick white cloudy liquid, which has no smell. It generally exits after one urinates and occasionally before.

wājib an obligation established by a speculative text (for more detail see 1.1).

waqf endowment.

wuḍū' ablution.

Bibliography

Aḥmad, Rashīḍ, *Aḥsan al-Fatāwā*. H. M. Sa[c]īd Company, 1994.

Aini, B, *al-Bināya sharḥ al-hidāya*, Dār al-fikr: Beirut 1990.

Ali, Mukhtār, *Ashraf al-Īḍāḥ sharḥ nūr al-īḍāḥ*. Kutub Khāna Mazharī: Karachi, 1996.

Al-Shāshī, Ibrahīm, *Uṣūl al-Shāshī*. Mīr Muḥammad Kutub Khāna: n.p., n.d.

Al-Zuhayly, Wahbah, *Al-fiqh al-Islāmī wa adillatuh*. Dār al-fikr 1989.

Ṭaḥtāwī, Aḥmad b. Muḥammad, *Hāshīya ala marāqī al-falāḥ sharḥ nūr al-īḍāḥ*. Egypt: n.d.

Lucknawī, [c]Abd al-Ḥai. *Al-ta[c]līq al-mumajjad [c]alā Muwaṭṭā Muḥammad*. Dar al-Qalam: Damascus, 1991.

Lucknawī, [c]Abd al-Ḥay, *al-raf[c] wa takmīl fī al-jarḥ wa al-ta[c]dīl*. Maktaba al-Maṭbū[c]āṭ al-Islāmīya: Beirut, 1987.

Keller, Nuḥ Ḥa Mīm. *Reliance of the Traveller*. Sunna Books: Evanston, 1994.

Khān, Sarfarāz, *Maqām Abī Ḥanīfa*. Maktaba Safdarīya: Pakistan 1993.

Kāndehlawī, Zakarīya, *al-Kanz al-matawārī,* Pakistan 1998.

Nawawi, Muhyu al-Din, *Sharḥ ṣaḥīḥ Muslim.* Dar al-Qalam: Beirut, 1987.

Ibn al-Hummām, Burhan al-Din, *Sharḥ fatḥ al-qadīr.* Dār al-Fikr: Beirut, n.d.

Makdasi, George, *The Non-Ashāʿrite Shāfiʿism of Abū Hāmid Ghazālī. Revue des Etudes,* 1986.

INDEX

G

H

I

J

K

L

M

N

O

P

Q

R

S

T

U

V

W

Z